my
sad
captains

my
sad
captains
and
other
poems
by
thom
gunn

THE
UNIVERSITY · OF CHICAGO
PRESS

Acknowledgments are made to the follow-
ing periodicals, in which these poems first
appeared: London Magazine, Encounter,
Poetry, Observer, Spectator, Paris Re-
view, Listen, Carleton Miscellany, Crit-
ical Quarterly; and also to The Bodley
Head, Ltd., for permission to quote from
The Last Tycoon, by F. Scott Fitzgerald.
Two Old English words are used in the
twelfth poem: *byrnies* were chain-mail
shirts, and a *nicker* was a water-monster.

Library of Congress Catalog Number: 61-15933

THE UNIVERSITY OF CHICAGO PRESS, CHICAGO 60637

Faber and Faber Limited, London W.C. 1, England

© 1961 by Thom Gunn. All rights reserved

Published 1961. Third Impression 1967

Printed in the United States of America

CONTENTS

Part 1

Part 2

1

The will is infinite
and the execution confined,
the desire is boundless
and the act a slave to limit.

<small>TROILUS AND CRESSIDA</small>

IN SANTA MARIA DEL POPOLO

Waiting for when the sun an hour or less
Conveniently oblique makes visible
The painting on one wall of this recess
By Caravaggio, of the Roman School,
I see how shadow in the painting brims
With a real shadow, drowning all shapes out
But a dim horse's haunch and various limbs,
Until the very subject is in doubt.

But evening gives the act, beneath the horse
And one indifferent groom, I see him sprawl,
Foreshortened from the head, with hidden face,
Where he has fallen, Saul becoming Paul.
O wily painter, limiting the scene
From a cacophany of dusty forms
To the one convulsion, what is it you mean
In that wide gesture of the lifting arms?

No Ananias croons a mystery yet,
Casting the pain out under name of sin.
The painter saw what was, an alternate
Candor and secrecy inside the skin.
He painted, elsewhere, that firm insolent
Young whore in Venus' clothes, those pudgy cheats,
Those sharpers; and was strangled, as things went,
For money, by one such picked off the streets.

I turn, hardly enlightened, from the chapel
To the dim interior of the church instead,
In which there kneel already several people,
Mostly old women: each head closeted
In tiny fists holds comfort as it can.
Their poor arms are too tired for more than this
—For the large gesture of solitary man,
Resisting, by embracing, nothingness.

THE ANNIHILATION OF NOTHING

Nothing remained: Nothing, the wanton name
That nightly I rehearsed till led away
To a dark sleep, or sleep that held one dream.

In this a huge contagious absence lay,
More space than space, over the cloud and slime,
Defined but by the encroachments of its sway.

Stripped to indifference at the turns of time,
Whose end I knew, I woke without desire,
And welcomed zero as a paradigm.

But now it breaks—images burst with fire
Into the quiet sphere where I have bided,
Showing the landscape holding yet entire:

The power that I envisaged, that presided
Ultimate in its abstract devastations,
Is merely change, the atoms it divided

Complete, in ignorance, new combinations.
Only an infinite finitude I see
In those peculiar lovely variations.

It is despair that nothing cannot be
Flares in the mind and leaves a smoky mark
Of dread.
              Look upward. Neither firm nor free,

Purposeless matter hovers in the dark.

THE MONSTER

I left my room at last, I walked
The streets of that decaying town,
I took the turn I had renounced
Where the carved cherub crumbled down.

Eager as to a granted wish
I hurried to the cul de sac.
Forestalled by whom? Before the house
I saw an unmoved waiting back.

How had she never vainly mentioned
This lover, too, unsatisfied?
Did she dismiss one every night?
I walked up slowly to his side.

Those eyes glazed like her windowpane,
That wide mouth ugly with despair,
Those arms held tight against the haunches,
Poised, but heavily staying there:

At once I knew him, gloating over
A grief defined and realized,
And living only for its sake.
It was myself I recognized.

I could not watch her window now,
Standing before this man of mine,
The constant one I had created
Lest the pure feeling should decline.

What if I were within the house,
Happier than the fact had been
—Would he, then, still be gazing here,
The man who never can get in?

Or would I, leaving at the dawn
A suppler love than he could guess,
Find him awake on my small bed,
Demanding still some bitterness?

THE MIDDLE OF THE NIGHT

Open, box, for the child
Who lifts out, one by one,
Impudent and self-willed
Dolls from the living heap
—Their antics never done
Which took him from his sleep.

Lion and citizen,
Soldier in pose of fight,
A wicker stork, small men,
Small gods and animals. . . .
The box is emptied out:
The floor is bright with dolls.

Year after year the same,
A town of perfect size.
Who calls it a mere game?
Round him, alive and shrunk
Each finished burgher lies,
Whose cargoes have been sunk.

He learns their histories—
Jerk, posture, giggle, prance,
And grows to recognize
In each doll, passive, faded,
Some man who is at once
Transfigured and degraded.

At length he writes it down,
Recording what befalls
Until the dark is gone.
Children who know by heart
The vices of their dolls
Will stay awake at night.

READINGS IN FRENCH

I

Refining Mallarmé at last destroyed
Flesh, passion, and their consequent confusions;
His poetry continued in a void
Where only furniture could have illusions.

II

Though Edgar Poë writes a lucid prose,
Just and rhetorical without exertion,
It loses all lucidity, God knows,
In the single, poorly-rendered English version.

III

Nothing Unusual about Marcel Proust
All are unmasked as perverts sooner or later,
With a notable exception—the narrator.

IV

L'Éducation Sentimentale
Mme. Arnoux is finely never there.
That is the point: the fineness, the despair.

V

Nausea fills me, and the only essence
Is in my tangible illegal presence.
I start from here. But where then did I learn
The terms that pose the choices I discern?

FROM THE HIGHEST CAMP

Nothing in this bright region melts or shifts.
The local names are concepts: the Ravine,
Pemmican Ridge, North Col, Death Camp, they mean
The streetless rise, the dazzling abstract drifts,
To which particular names adhere by chance,
From custom lightly, not from character.
We stand on a white terrace and confer;
This is the last camp of experience.

What is that sudden yelp upon the air?
And whose are these cold droppings? whose malformed
Purposeless tracks about the slope? We know.
The abominable endures, existing where
Nothing else can: it is—unfed, unwarmed—
Born of rejection, of the boundless snow.

INNOCENCE

(for Tony White)

He ran the course and as he ran he grew,
And smelt his fragrance in the field. Already,
Running he knew the most he ever knew,
The egotism of a healthy body.

Ran into manhood, ignorant of the past:
Culture of guilt and guilt's vague heritage,
Self-pity and the soul; what he possessed
Was rich, potential, like the bud's tipped rage.

The Corps developed, it was plain to see,
Courage, endurance, loyalty and skill
To a morale firm as morality,
Hardening him to an instrument, until

The finitude of virtues that were there
Bodied within the swarthy uniform
A compact innocence, child-like and clear,
No doubt could penetrate, no act could harm.

When he stood near the Russian partisan
Being burned alive, he therefore could behold
The ribs wear gently through the darkening skin
And sicken only at the Northern cold,

Could watch the fat burn with a violet flame
And feel disgusted only at the smell,
And judge that all pain finishes the same
As melting quietly by his boots it fell.

MODES OF PLEASURE

I jump with terror seeing him,
Dredging the bar with that stiff glare
As fiercely as if each whim there
Were passion, whose passion is a whim:

The Fallen Rake, being fallen from
The heights of twenty to middle age,
And helpless to control his rage,
So mean, so few the chances come.

The very beauty of his prime
Was that the triumphs which recurred
In different rooms without a word
Would all be lost some time in time.

Thus he reduced the wild unknown.
And having used each hour of leisure
To learn by rote the modes of pleasure,
The sensual skills as skills alone,

He knows that nothing, not the most
Cunning or sweet, can hold him, still.
Living by habit of the will,
He cannot contemplate the past,

Cannot discriminate, condemned
To the sharpest passion of them all.
Rigid he sits: brave, terrible,
The will awaits its gradual end.

MODES OF PLEASURE

New face, strange face, for my unrest.
I hunt your look, and lust marks time
Dark in his doubtful uniform,
Preparing once more for the test.

You do not know you are observed:
Apart, contained, you wait on chance,
Or seem to, till your callous glance
Meets mine, as callous and reserved.

And as it does we recognize
That sharing an anticipation
Amounts to a collaboration—
A warm game for a warmer prize.

Yet when I've had you once or twice
I may not want you any more:
A single night is plenty for
Every magnanimous device.

Why should that matter? Why pretend
Love must accompany erection?
This is a momentary affection,
A curiosity bound to end,

Which as good-humored muscle may
Against the muscle try its strength
—Exhausted into sleep at length—
And will not last long into day.

A MAP OF THE CITY

I stand upon a hill and see
A luminous country under me,
Through which at two the drunk must weave;
The transient's pause, the sailor's leave.

I notice, looking down the hill,
Arms braced upon a window sill;
And on the web of fire escapes
Move the potential, the grey shapes.

I hold the city here, complete:
And every shape defined by light
Is mine, or corresponds to mine,
Some flickering or some steady shine.

This map is ground of my delight.
Between the limits, night by night,
I watch a malady's advance,
I recognize my love of chance.

By the recurrent lights I see
Endless potentiality,
The crowded, broken, and unfinished!
I would not have the risk diminished.

THE BOOK OF THE DEAD

The blood began to waste into the clods.
Meanwhile his soldiers kept the dead away
At sword-point, though some clamored by the gods,
And some by friendship—hard, hard to deny.

Slowly the form took body; they could see
Blood flow down the diaphanous throat, slow, stay,
Clot, till the neck became opaque. And he,
Tiresias, stood before them, heavy as they.

What comfort could he bring them? (Circling past,
Poor, drained of cunning, they would also grope
After a goat's blood even.) Might the last
Action of which he spoke be ground for hope?
But winnowing is one action out of many.
After the winnowing, you must grind, bake, eat,
And then once more turn out into the rainy
Acres to plough, your mantle weighing wet
Round your swaddled ankles, your knuckles raw, your
    cheek
Fretted with tiny veins,—and not assured
That it will be, this time, either easier work
Or more successful. Even, perhaps, more hard.

Yet by the time Odysseus saw the throat,
Guttering, whiten, he was glad. The dead
Desire what they can never bring about;
The living bring discriminate gifts of blood,
Clumsily, wasting far more than they give,
But able still to bring. He knew the lack,
And watching, without comfort, was alive
Because he had no comfort. He turned back.

THE BYRNIES

The heroes paused upon the plain.
When one of them but swayed, ring mashed on ring:
   Sound of the byrnie's knitted chain,
Vague evocations of the constant Thing.

They viewed beyond a salty hill
Barbaric forest, mesh of branch and root
   —A huge obstruction growing still,
Darkening the land, in quietness absolute.

That dark was fearful—lack of presence—
Unless some man could chance upon or win
   Magical signs to stay the essence
Of the broad light that they adventured in.

Elusive light of light that went
Flashing on water, edging round a mass,
   Inching across fat stems, or spent
Lay thin and shrunk among the bristling grass.

Creeping from sense to craftier sense,
Acquisitive, and loss their only fear,
   These men had fashioned a defence
Against the nicker's snap, and hostile spear.

Byrnie on byrnie! as they turned
They saw light trapped between the man-made joints,
   Central in every link it burned,
Reduced and steadied to a thousand points.

Thus for each blunt-faced ignorant one
The great grey rigid uniform combined
    Safety with virtue of the sun.
Thus concepts linked like chainmail in the mind.

    Reminded, by the grinding sound,
Of what they sought, and partly understood,
    They paused upon that open ground,
A little group above the foreign wood.

BLACK JACKETS

In the silence that prolongs the span
Rawly of music when the record ends,
   The red-haired boy who drove a van
In weekday overalls but, like his friends,

   Wore cycle boots and jacket here
To suit the Sunday hangout he was in,
   Heard, as he stretched back from his beer,
Leather creak softly round his neck and chin.

Before him, on a coal-black sleeve
Remote exertion had lined, scratched, and burned
   Insignia that could not revive
The heroic fall or climb where they were earned.

On the other drinkers bent together,
Concocting selves for their impervious kit,
   He saw it as no more than leather
Which, taut across the shoulders grown to it,

Sent through the dimness of a bar
As sudden and anonymous hints of light
   As those that shipping give, that are
Now flickers in the Bay, now lost in night.

He stretched out like a cat, and rolled
The bitterish taste of beer upon his tongue,
   And listened to a joke being told:
The present was the things he stayed among.

If it was only loss he wore,
He wore it to assert, with fierce devotion,
    Complicity and nothing more.
He recollected his initiation,

    And one especially of the rites.
For on his shoulders they had put tattoos:
    The group's name on the left, The Knights,
And on the right the slogan Born To Lose.

BAUDELAIRE AMONG THE HEROES

Charles Baudelaire knew that the human heart
Associates with not the whole but part.
The parts are fetishes: invariable
Particularities which furnish hell.

THE VALUE OF GOLD

The hairs turn gold upon my thigh,
And I am gold beneath the sun,
Losing pale features that the cold
Pinched, pointed, for an instant I
Turn blind to features, being one
With all that has, like me, turned gold.

I finish up the can of beer,
And lay my head on the cropped grass:
Now bordering flag, geranium,
And mint-bush tower above me here,
Which color into color pass
Toward the last state they shall become.

Of insect size, I walk below
The red, green, greenish-black, and black,
And speculate. Can this quiet growth
Comprise at once the still-to-grow
And a full form without a lack?
And, if so, can I too be both?

I darken where perpetual
Action withdraws me from the sun.
Then from one high precocious stalk
A flower—its fulness reached—lets fall
Features, great petals, one by one
Shrivelling to gold across my walk.

CLAUS VON STAUFFENBERG

of the bomb-plot on Hitler, 1944

What made the place a landscape of despair,
History stunned beneath, the emblems cracked?
Smell of approaching snow hangs on the air;
The frost meanwhile can be the only fact.

They chose the unknown, and the bounded terror,
As a corrective, who corrected live
Surveying without choice the bounding error:
An unsanctioned present must be primitive.

A few still have the vigor to deny
Fear is a natural state; their motives neither
Of doctrinaire, of turncoat, nor of spy.
Lucidity of thought draws them together.

The maimed young Colonel who can calculate
On two remaining fingers and a will,
Takes lessons from the past, to detonate
A bomb that Brutus rendered possible.

Over the maps a moment, face to face:
Across from Hitler, whose grey eyes have filled
A nation with the illogic of their gaze,
The rational man is poised, to break, to build.

And though he fails, honor personified
In a cold time where honor cannot grow,
He stiffens, like a statue, in mid-stride
—Falling toward history, and under snow.

2

I looked back as we crossed the crest of the foothills—with the air so clear you could see the leaves on Sunset Mountains two miles away. It's startling to you sometimes—just air, unobstructed, uncomplicated air.

'The Last Tycoon,' F. Scott Fitsgerald

WAKING IN A NEWLY-BUILT HOUSE

The window, a wide pane in the bare
modern wall, is crossed by colorless
peeling trunks of the eucalyptus
recurring against raw sky-color.

It wakes me, and my eyes rest on it,
sharpening, and seeking merely all
of what can be seen, the substantial,
where the things themselves are adequate.

So I observe them, able to see
them as they are, the neutral sections
of trunk, spare, solid, lacking at once
disconnectedness and unity.

There is a tangible remoteness
of the air about me, its clean chill
ordering every room of the hill-
top house, and convoking absences.

Calmly, perception rests on the things,
and is aware of them only in
their precise definition, their fine
lack of even potential meanings.

FLYING ABOVE CALIFORNIA

Spread beneath me it lies—lean upland
sinewed and tawny in the sun, and

valley cool with mustard, or sweet with
loquat. I repeat under my breath

names of places I have not been to:
Crescent City, San Bernardino

—Mediterranean and Northern names.
Such richness can make you drunk. Sometimes

on fogless days by the Pacific,
there is a cold hard light without break

that reveals merely what is—no more
and no less. That limiting candor,

that accuracy of the beaches,
is part of the ultimate richness.

CONSIDERING THE SNAIL

The snail pushes through a green
night, for the grass is heavy
with water and meets over
the bright path he makes, where rain
has darkened the earth's dark. He
moves in a wood of desire,

pale antlers barely stirring
as he hunts. I cannot tell
what power is at work, drenched there
with purpose, knowing nothing.
What is a snail's fury? All
I think is that if later

I parted the blades above
the tunnel and saw the thin
trail of broken white across
litter, I would never have
imagined the slow passion
to that deliberate progress.

"BLACKIE, THE ELECTRIC REMBRANDT"

We watch through the shop-front while
Blackie draws stars—an equal

concentration on his and
the youngster's faces. The hand

is steady and accurate;
but the boy does not see it

for his eyes follow the point
that touches (quick, dark movement!)

a virginal arm beneath
his rolled sleeve: he holds his breath.

. . . Now that it is finished, he
hands a few bills to Blackie

and leaves with a bandage on
his arm, under which gleam ten

stars, hanging in a blue thick
cluster. Now he is starlike.

HOTBLOOD ON FRIDAY

Expectant yet relaxed, he
basks within the body's tight
limits, the tender reaches;
and acquires by street-light the
details which accumulate
to a sense of crude richness

that almost unseats reason.
At last, the present! His step
springs on the sidewalk like a
voice of appetite. The town
is gradually opening up,
this as on every Friday:

stone petals bright in the warm
evening. No hand can grasp it.
Quick, Hotblood, in the boisterous
community find some term,
precarious and accurate,
that assumes it without loss.

THE FEEL OF HANDS

The hands explore tentatively,
two small live entities whose shapes
I have to guess at. They touch me
all, with the light of fingertips

testing each surface of each thing
found, timid as kittens with it.
I connect them with amusing
hands I have shaken by daylight.

There is a sudden transition:
they plunge together in a full
formed single fury; they are grown
to cats, hunting without scruple;

they are expert but desperate.
I am in the dark. I wonder
when they grew up. It strikes me that
I do not know whose hands they are.

L'ÉPREUVE

(for *Paul Bowles*)

I

My body trots semblably
on Market Street. I control
that thick and singular spy
from a hovering planet: I
contemplate new laws meanwhile.

According to which it is
not a thoroughfare below
but a sweet compact. I choose
as if for the first time this
as the world I'll come back to.

II

Not yet. I am distinct. I
am now afflicted with thirst
heat and cold, bombarded by
rockets that explode greenly,
harried by shapes, cramped. The worst

is, I am still on my own.
The street's total is less near
during my long ordeal than
the turbanned legends within
my world of serried color.

RASTIGNAC AT 45

Here he is of course. It was his best
trick always: when we glance again toward
the shadow we see it has consist-
ed of him all along, lean and bored.

We denounced him so often! Yet he
comes up, and leans on one of the bars
in his dark suit, indicating the
empty glass as if we were waiters.

We fill it, and submit, more or less,
to his marvellous air of knowing
all the ropes debonair weariness
could care to handle, of "everything

that I know I know from having done,
child, and I survive." What calmly told
confidences of exploration
among the oversexed and titled,

or request for a few days' loan, are
we about to hear? Rastignac tell us
about Life, and what men of your
stamp endure. It must be terrible.

It is. To the left of his mouth is
an attractive scarlike line, not caused
by time unhelped. It is not the prize,
either, of a dueller's lucky thrust.

But this: time after time the fetid
taste to the platitudes of Romance
has drawn his mouth up to the one side
secretly, in a half-maddened wince.

We cannot help but pity him that
momentary convulsion; however,
the mere custom of living with it
has, for him, diminished the horror.

LIGHTS AMONG REDWOOD

of Muir Woods

And the streams here, ledge to ledge,
take care of light. Only to
the pale green ribs of young ferns
tangling above the creek's edge
it may sometimes escape, though
in quick diffusing patterns.

Elsewhere it has become tone,
pure and rarified; at most
a muted dimness colored
with moss-green, charred grey, leaf-brown.
Calm shadow! Then we at last
remember to look upward:

constant, to laws of size and
age the thick forms hold, though gashed
through with Indian fires. At once
tone is forgotten: we stand
and stare—mindless, diminished—
at their rosy immanence.

ADOLESCENCE

After the history has been made,
and when Wallace's shaggy head

glares on London from a spike, when
the exiled general is again

gliding into Athens harbor
now as embittered foreigner,

when the lean creatures crawl out of
camps and in silence try to live;

I pass foundations of houses,
walking through the wet spring, my knees

drenched from high grass charged with water,
and am part, still, of the done war.

A TRUCKER

Sometimes it is like a beast
barely controlled by a man.
But the cabin is lofty
as a skull, and all the rest
extends from his foot as an
enormous throbbing body:

if he left anything to
chance—see his great frame capsize,
and his rubber limbs explode
whirling! and see there follow
a bright fountain of red eyes
tinkling sightless to the road.

LOOT

I

I am approaching. Past dry
towers softly seeding from mere
delicacy of age, I
penetrate, through thickets, or

over warm herbs my feet press
to brief potency. Now with
the green quickness of grasses
mingles the smell of the earth,

raw and black. I am about
to raid the earth and open
again those low chambers that
wary fathers stand guard in.

II

Poised on hot walls I try to
imagine them caught beneath
in the village, in shadow:
I can almost hear them breathe.

This time what shall I take? Powers
hidden and agile, yield now
value: here, uniquely yours.
Direct me. But dark below

in the boneworks, you only
move in time with my pulse, and
observe without passion the
veer of my impassioned mind.

III

This. Hands numb from sifting soil
I find at last a trinket
carved whole from some mineral:
nameless and useless thing that

is for me to name and use.
But even as I relax my
fingers round its cool surface,
I am herald to tawny

warriors, woken from sleep, who
ride precipitantly down
with the blood toward my hands, through
me to retain possession.

MY SAD CAPTAINS

One by one they appear in
the darkness: a few friends, and
a few with historical
names. How late they start to shine!
but before they fade they stand
perfectly embodied, all

the past lapping them like a
cloak of chaos. They were men
who, I thought, lived only to
renew the wasteful force they
spent with each hot convulsion.
They remind me, distant now.

True, they are not at rest yet,
but now that they are indeed
apart, winnowed from failures,
they withdraw to an orbit
and turn with disinterested
hard energy, like the stars.